Energy Resources Around the World

by Samantha Beres

Table of Contents

Introduction	2
Chapter 1: Fossil Fuels	4
Chapter 2: Nuclear Energy	14
Chapter 3: Hydropower	18
Chapter 4: Solar, Wind, Geothermal, and Biomass Energy	22
Conclusion	30
Glossary	31
Index	32

Can you imagine a day without electricity? We couldn't use our computers or our televisions. Forget about a nighttime football game! There would be no way to light the field. Imagine that same day without gasoline. Cars and school buses would be useless.

We use different kinds of energy to light our houses, to power our cars, and for many other reasons. Energy resources are the raw materials we use to produce energy. For example, the energy resource for gasoline is oil. The energy resource used to produce electricity might be coal or wind power. Some energy resources can't be replaced once they've been used up. They are called **nonrenewable resources.** The supply of these resources is limited. This means we could run out of them someday. Oil, coal, and natural gas are nonrenewable. As you read, look for how nonrenewable energy resources were formed and how they're used.

Some energy resources are continually renewed or replaced. They are called **renewable resources.** Water, the Sun, and the wind are renewable energy resources.

In this book, you'll learn about both nonrenewable and renewable energy resources. You'll learn which are used the most and how each type affects the environment.

IT'S A FACT

A watt is a unit of electric power. The electrical energy we use is measured in watt-hours. For example, a 60-watt light bulb uses 60 watts of power in one hour.

To measure larger amounts of energy, we use kilowatts (1,000 watts). The average American household uses about 1,000 kilowatt-hours (or 1 million watt-hours) of electricity every month! To measure even greater amounts of energy, we use megawatts (1 million watts) and gigawatts (1 billion watts).

The gasoline that fuels most vehicles comes from a nonrenewable energy resource.

CHAPTER 1

Fossil Fuels

Oil, coal, and natural gas are **fossil fuels**. All the fossil fuels are nonrenewable energy resources.

You use fossil fuels every day. Oil is refined, or made pure, to make gasoline for many kinds of vehicles, including cars, boats, and planes. Oil is also burned to heat homes. Oil, coal, and natural gas are burned to generate electricity. Natural gas is used for cooking and to heat homes.

Fossil fuels started forming about 300 million years ago, long before the

an oil refinery

age of dinosaurs. Back then, Earth was covered with swamps and oceans.

When the plants and other organisms living in these waters died, they sank to the bottom. In time, the dead matter was buried under sediment—layers of sand and mud.

Over millions of years, pressure from the layers above and Earth's heat below changed the sediment into rock. In turn, the pressure of the rock and sediment changed the dead matter into fossil fuels.

Sources of Fossil Fuels

This table shows the sources of different fossil fuels.

Fossil Fuel	Source
oil	one-celled organisms, marine plants
coal	trees, ferns, mosses
natural gas	algae (AL-jee)—tiny plants that live in water

CHAPTER 1

Fossil fuel deposits are deep underground. Deposits of oil and natural gas are often found near fractured places, or cracks, in the ground called fault lines. Oil and natural gas can move along these cracks and collect in pools.

Deposits of oil and natural gas are also found under the ocean floor. This is why we see oil and natural gas drilling platforms offshore in some places.

Energy companies spend a lot of time and money searching for fossil fuel deposits. Deposits that have been found but not yet taken out of the ground are called fuel **reserves**.

an oil-drilling platform

Careers in SCIENCE

Geologists are scientists who study rock formations to learn about the history of Earth. Oil and gas companies often hire geologists to study rock formations to learn the locations of fossil fuels. Geologists take courses in mathematics and science. A Master's degree is usually the minimum educational requirement for the job. Most high-level research positions require a Ph.D. degree.

This geologist is using equipment to explore underground rock layers. The information he gathers is used to locate oil deposits.

FOSSIL FUELS

Oil

Oil is obtained by drilling deep into an oil reserve and pumping the oil out. Pipelines then carry the oil to ships and to oil refineries.

Fifty-five percent of the world's oil reserves are in the Middle East. The United States also has oil reserves, but not enough to meet its needs. The United States imports more than half of the oil it uses.

Depending on oil from other countries can cause problems. For example, conflicts in the Middle East can limit the amount of oil that is produced there.

IT'S A FACT

The Trans-Alaska Pipeline is one of the longest oil pipelines in the world. It runs 800 miles (1,287.44 kilometers) from Prudhoe Bay to the port of Valdez. Each month, 47,000 gallons (213,666 liters) of oil flow through it.

Because much of the ground in Alaska is frozen, about half the pipeline is above ground. In more than 500 places, the pipeline is at least 10 feet high to allow animals to pass under it.

When less oil is available, its price goes up. Then the costs of home heating oil and gasoline go up, too.

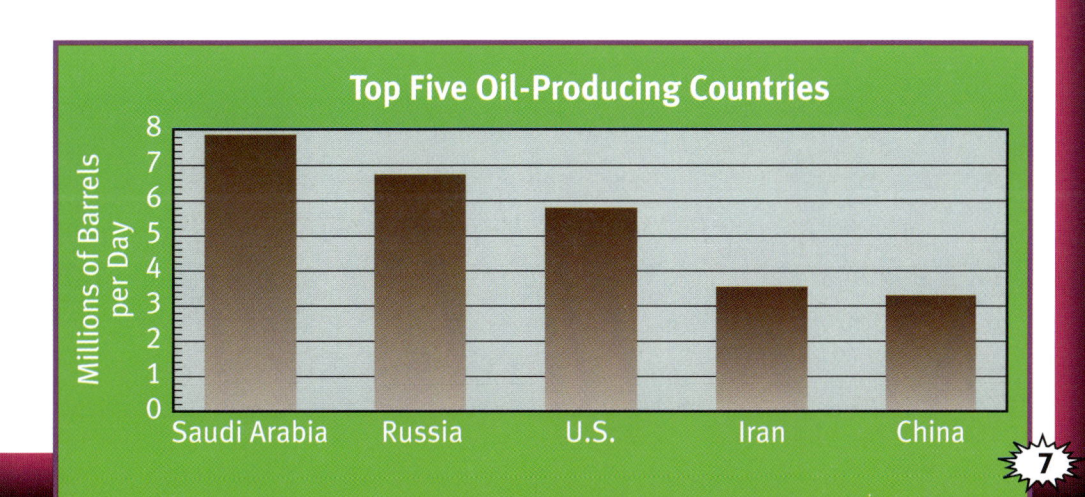

Top Five Oil-Producing Countries

(Millions of Barrels per Day)

Country	Saudi Arabia	Russia	U.S.	Iran	China
Barrels	~8	~7	~6	~3.5	~3.5

CHAPTER 1

Natural Gas

Like oil, natural gas is obtained by drilling deep into underground reserves. Oil and natural gas are often found together. Natural gas is lighter than oil, so it floats above the oil.

Russia has the most natural gas reserves of any country. The Middle East is also rich in natural gas. This region holds nearly one-third of the world's reserves. The United States is the leader in natural gas production. It produces most of the natural gas it uses.

a natural gas refinery in Kansas

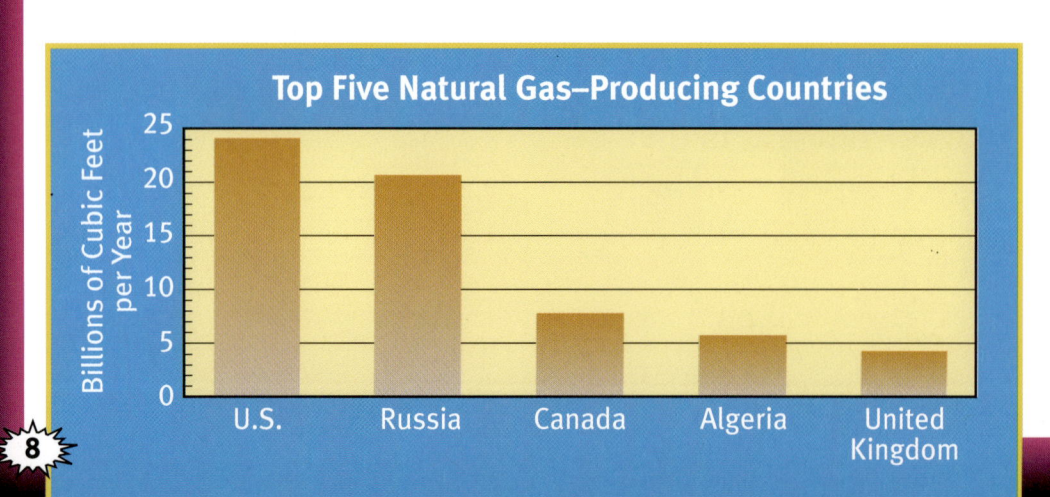

Top Five Natural Gas–Producing Countries

Billions of Cubic Feet per Year

U.S.	~24
Russia	~20
Canada	~7
Algeria	~6
United Kingdom	~4

8

FOSSIL FUELS

IT'S A FACT

For many years, natural gas was considered a waste product of oil production and was burned off!

> Natural gas is used to fuel gas stoves.

Of all the fossil fuels, natural gas burns the cleanest. It causes less pollution when burned than oil and coal do. In the United States, natural gas is also one of the cheapest fossil fuels. Although its price has gone up in the last few years, natural gas is still one of the least expensive ways to heat your home. Six in ten homes in the United States are heated by natural gas.

Because natural gas is cheap and less polluting than oil and coal, many plants that generate electricity burn natural gas. Many plants that now burn oil and coal are likely to convert to natural gas.

CHAPTER 1

Coal

Like oil and natural gas, coal is found underground. It is mined, or dug out of the ground. Over the last 100 years, coal mining has gone through many changes. People used to dig the coal using simple tools. Now modern machinery helps with a lot of the work.

Coal is mined in more than 50 countries. China is the largest producer of coal in the world. The United States mines coal in more than 20 states and is the second largest producer in the world. About 40 percent of the world's electricity is generated by burning coal.

IT'S A FACT

In the early days of coal mining in the United States, children sometimes worked in the mines. Some of them were as young as six years old! Many of the children were orphans. Often they worked for 12 to 18 hours a day with little to eat.

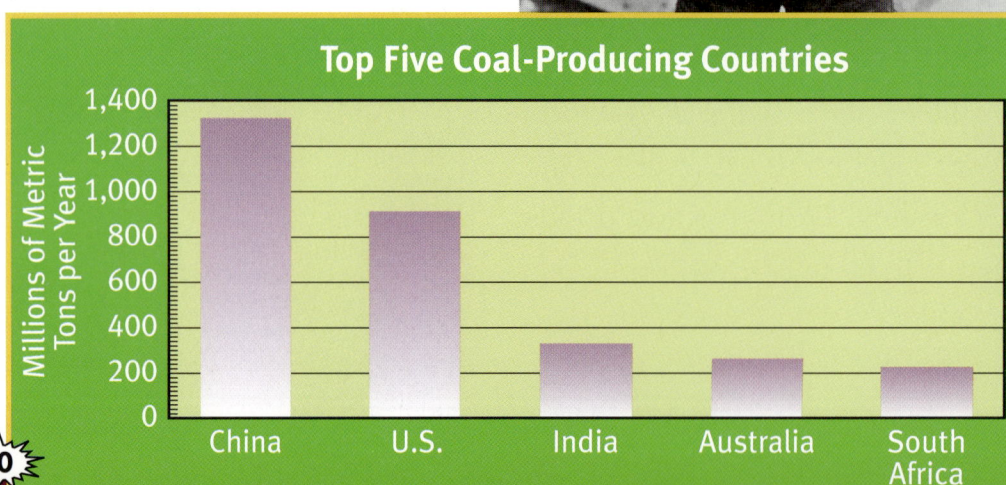

Top Five Coal-Producing Countries

Country	Millions of Metric Tons per Year
China	~1,320
U.S.	~910
India	~330
Australia	~250
South Africa	~220

Problems with Fossil Fuels

Fossil fuels now provide about 90 percent of the world's energy. But the supply of fossil fuels is limited. In the future, we will probably need to rely on other sources of energy.

There's another possible problem with fossil fuels. Burning fossil fuels releases carbon dioxide, one of many greenhouse gases. Like a glass greenhouse, these gases trap heat. With too many greenhouse gases in the atmosphere, some scientists think that Earth might become too warm. This is called global warming. Global warming might cause many serious problems. It could cause droughts in some places. If polar ice melts, the sea level could rise and cause flooding. Droughts and floods would affect our water supplies and crops.

✓ Point

Read More About It

You can read more about problems with fossil fuels at your school media center or local library. An adult can help you search the Internet for information.

An arctic fox crosses polar ice. Some scientists think global warming might melt polar ice.

CHAPTER 1

Factories, power plants, and cars that burn fossil fuels send harmful **emissions** into the air. (Smoke is a kind of emission.) To improve air quality, the United States created a law called the Clean Air Act. This law sets limits on the amount of emissions that are allowed.

In some states, cars have to pass emissions tests on a regular basis. Factories and power plants use filters to capture emissions before they go into the air. Devices called "scrubbers" at coal-burning power plants clean the smoke that leaves smokestacks. Scrubbers can cut emissions by 90 percent.

Science in the News

Can a car run on french-fry grease? It can if it has a fry-grease engine converter. The converter allows a car with a diesel engine to run on fry grease from fast-food restaurants. This cuts down on the car's emissions. And filling up on fry grease is cheaper than using gas!

This van runs on fry grease instead of gasoline.

FOSSIL FUELS

Fossil fuels can cause pollution even before they are burned. Several oil tankers, or ships that transport oil, have had accidents. The tankers spilled the oil they were carrying. The spilled oil polluted the water and killed sea animals.

In 1989, an oil tanker named the *Exxon Valdez* ran aground in Alaska and broke open. It spilled 11 million gallons of oil into the ocean! The spill stretched for 460 miles (740 kilometers). Hundreds of thousands of sea birds, otters, and other animals were killed.

Thick oil floats on the ocean after an oil spill.

A man holds a bird covered with oil from the *Exxon Valdez* oil spill.

CHAPTER 2

Nuclear Energy

A metal called uranium (yer-AY-nee-uhm) is the source of nuclear energy. Uranium ore is mined from the ground. The uranium goes through several stages of processing before it is formed into small pellets.

Unlike fossil fuels, uranium pellets aren't burned to produce energy. Instead, uranium atoms in the pellets are split into smaller parts. When the atoms are split, a great deal of energy is released. This energy can be used to generate electricity.

IT'S A FACT

A one-inch uranium pellet generates about the same amount of electricity as one ton of coal.

an open-pit uranium mine in France

NUCLEAR ENERGY

The United States has more than 60 nuclear power plants. These plants provide 20 percent of the country's electricity. In France, nuclear energy provides almost 80 percent of the country's electricity. Around the world, more than 400 nuclear power plants are generating electricity.

Nuclear energy has some benefits. It costs less than fossil fuels and causes very little air pollution. It helps meet the growing demand for energy.

They Made a Difference

In 1966, scientist Lise Meitner (LEE-zuh MIGHT-ner) won an award from the U.S. Department of Energy for her work with uranium. Dr. Meitner observed and explained how uranium atoms split. She named this splitting of uranium atoms *fission*.

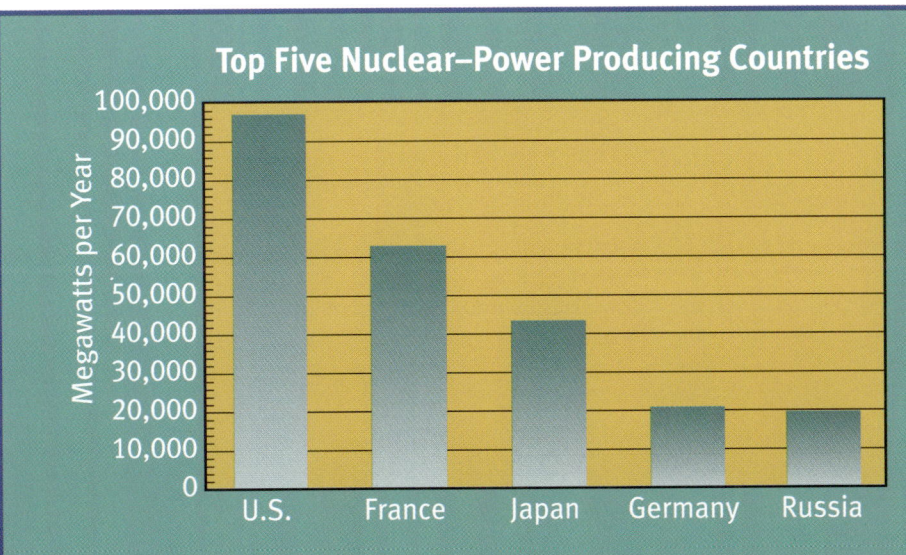

Top Five Nuclear-Power Producing Countries

Country	Megawatts per Year (approx.)
U.S.	97,000
France	63,000
Japan	43,000
Germany	21,000
Russia	20,000

Nuclear energy also has drawbacks. Although uranium is a nonrenewable resource, that is not its greatest drawback. One of the biggest problems is **radioactive waste**. After uranium pellets have been used, they and their storage containers emit harmful **radiation**. Large doses of radiation can cause cancer—even death. This waste remains radioactive for hundreds of thousands of years!

Where should we store nuclear waste? Countries around the world are trying to find answers to this question. Burying the waste is one possible answer. Shafts could be sunk deep into solid rock. After the shafts are filled with waste, they could be sealed. But getting the waste to the shaft could be very dangerous. What if a train or truck carrying nuclear waste were in an accident? The waste could spill and release very harmful radiation.

Three Mile Island nuclear power plant in Pennsylvania

NUCLEAR ENERGY

After the Chernobyl accident, a man uses a special device to check a car for radiation.

Accidents have occurred at nuclear power plants. In 1979, a serious problem occurred in one section of the Three Mile Island nuclear power plant in Pennsylvania. Luckily, no explosion took place. If it had, radioactive waste would have been blasted high into the air. Winds could have carried it for miles.

A terrible accident *did* occur on April 26, 1986, at the Chernobyl (cher-NOH-buhl) nuclear power plant in the country of Ukraine. During a test, there was a huge explosion in the plant. A gigantic fireball shot radioactive material into the air. More than 30,000 people had to leave their homes. More than 30 people died from radiation sickness or burns. Thousands of other people became sick.

CHAPTER 3

Hydropower

If you have ever seen a fast-moving river, you know that moving water has a lot of energy. The energy of moving water is used to generate power, or **hydropower**.

A hydropower plant starts with a dam being built on a river. Water from the river backs up behind the dam, forming a lake. The lake water then falls many feet through tunnels in the dam until it hits turbines. A turbine is like a wheel with blades. When the fast-moving, falling water hits the blades, the turbine turns. This spins a **generator**. The spinning generator produces electricity. About 20 percent of the world's electricity is generated this way.

Science in the News

China is building the Three Gorges Dam on the Yangtze (yang-SEE) River to make use of hydropower. China expects the dam to supply the same amount of energy as 18 nuclear plants or 40 million tons of coal.

HYDROPOWER

Hydropower can be produced wherever there is a large supply of moving water. Some places in the United States make good use of hydropower. The state of Washington has hydropower plants on the Columbia River that generate 87 percent of its electricity. But the United States as a whole uses hydropower for only 10 percent of its electrical needs.

The Grand Coulee Dam on the Columbia River, show below, is one of the largest hydropower dams in the country.

These turbines inside a dam on the Columbia River generate hydropower.

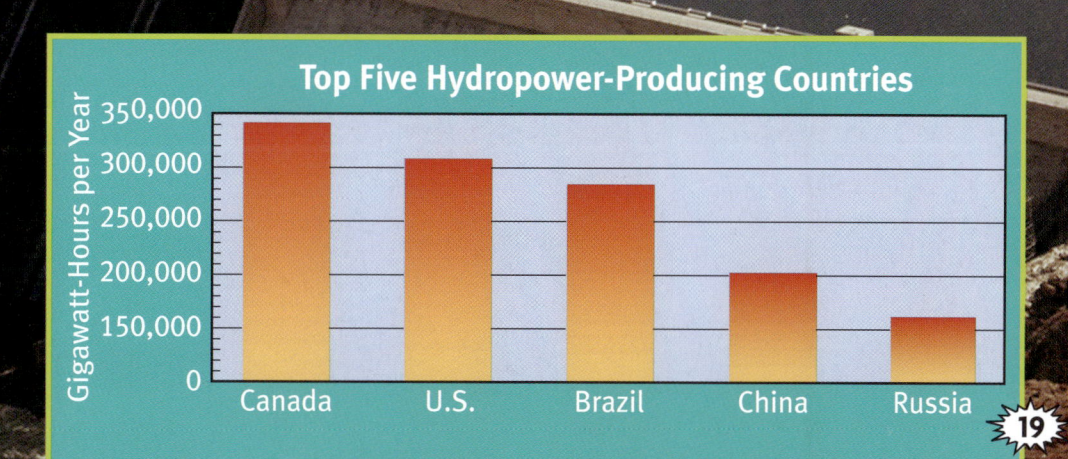

Top Five Hydropower-Producing Countries

Country	Gigawatt-Hours per Year
Canada	~340,000
U.S.	~305,000
Brazil	~280,000
China	~200,000
Russia	~160,000

In many ways, hydropower is ideal. Water is a renewable resource. Hydropower doesn't pollute the air, and it creates little waste. However, it can still harm the environment. A hydropower plant can affect the habitats of the birds, fish, and other animals that live near it.

Helping the Salmon

Hydropower dams can cause problems with salmon migration. Salmon migrate from the ocean into rivers to breed. Dams that block rivers keep the fish from reaching their breeding grounds. As a result, the number of salmon decreases.

One solution to the problem is building fish ladders. A fish ladder is a series of steps alongside a dam with water rushing over them. Salmon and other fish can get around the dam by going up and down these steps.

a fish ladder in Nevada

salmon leaping up the steps of a fish ladder

HYDROPOWER

statues outside one of the temples of Abu Simbel in Egypt

IT'S A FACT

In 1970, Egypt completed a dam across the Nile River at Aswan (a-SWAN). The dam controls the Nile's yearly floods and generates huge amounts of electricity. The lake formed by the dam threatened one of Egypt's ancient treasures—the temples of Abu Simbel (ah-boo SIHM-buhl). To save the temples, workers dug them out of their cliff and took them apart. Then they rebuilt them on high ground. The task took five years!

Dams can also cause problems for people. Building a dam creates a lake. What happens to people who live where the dam and its lake will be? They are displaced, or moved. China's Three Gorges Dam will displace more than a million people! Worldwide, about 80 million people have been displaced to make room for dams.

Another problem with dams is that they sometimes collapse and cause floods. In 1960, a dam in Brazil collapsed because of heavy rainfall. About 100,000 people had to be taken to safety. Half lost their homes in the flood.

CHAPTER 4

Solar, Wind, Geothermal and Biomass Energy

The Sun and the wind are both examples of renewable resources. Renewable resources won't run out the way fossil fuels might. Yet most places in the world don't rely very much on renewable resources. Why not?

One reason is cost. The technologies that generate energy from the Sun and the wind are costly. That makes it hard for people to switch from cheaper kinds of energy.

The good news is that the costs of these technologies are starting to fall. At the same time, the costs of fossil fuels are rising. Also, concern is growing about damage done to the environment by the use of fossil fuels. These factors could lead to greater use of renewable resources.

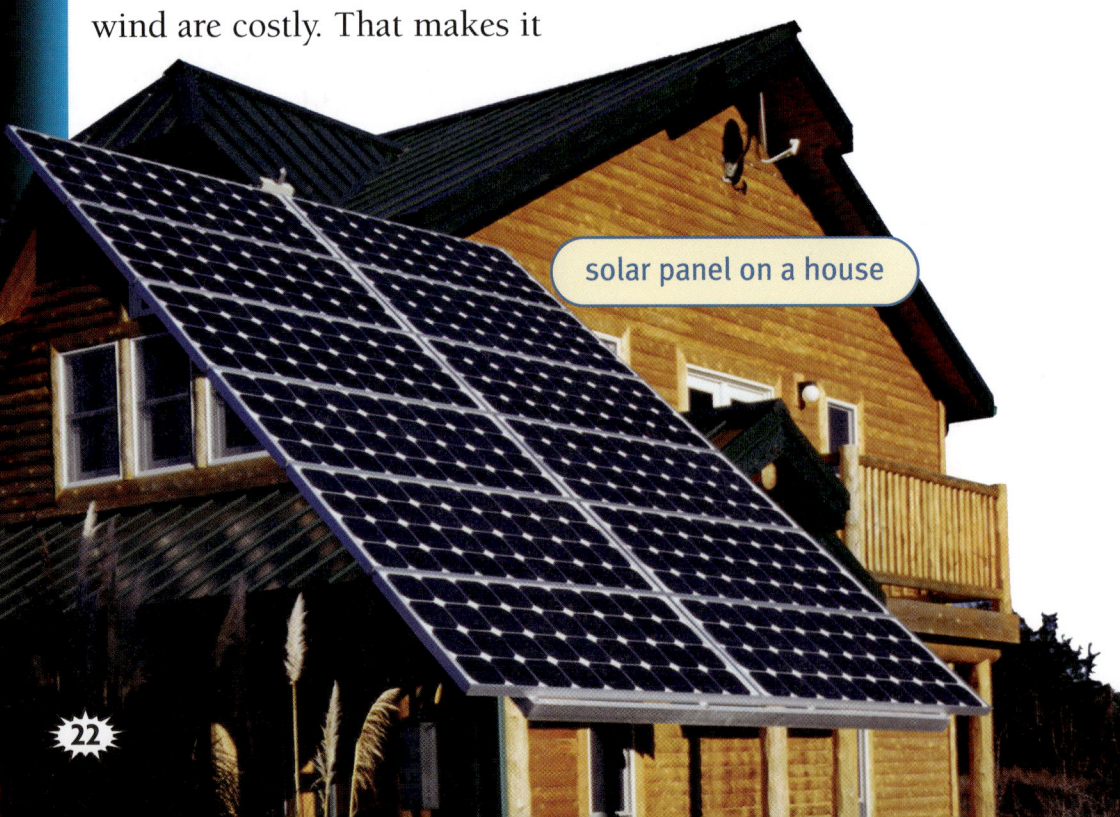

solar panel on a house

Some power plants convert energy from the Sun into electricity. These solar panels are absorbing sunlight at a solar power plant.

Solar Energy

Solar energy is energy from the Sun. Sunlight can be converted, or changed, into heat and electricity using solar cells. Have you ever seen a solar panel on a roof? The panel is made up of solar cells, also called photovoltaic (foh-toh-vawl-TAY-ihk) cells. The electricity the cells generate can be stored in batteries and used later.

More than 200,000 homes across the world rely on solar energy for all their electricity. Many of these homes are in rural areas far from a power plant. Because it would be expensive to run power lines to the homes, they rely on their own solar power systems instead.

CHAPTER 4

This car runs on solar energy.

Solar energy accounts for only one percent of the electricity produced worldwide. Why? Weather is one of the problems. The collection of solar energy is limited on cloudy or rainy days. Homes that rely on their own solar energy systems have a backup energy source for days with no sunshine.

Another problem is the high cost of solar energy systems. The governments of some countries have found ways to help people with these costs.

The German government offers low-interest loans to people who buy solar energy systems. Its "100,000 Roofs" program aims to put solar systems in 100,000 homes and businesses.

Japan has a similar program, as does the United States. The United States aims to put solar systems on one million roofs by the year 2010.

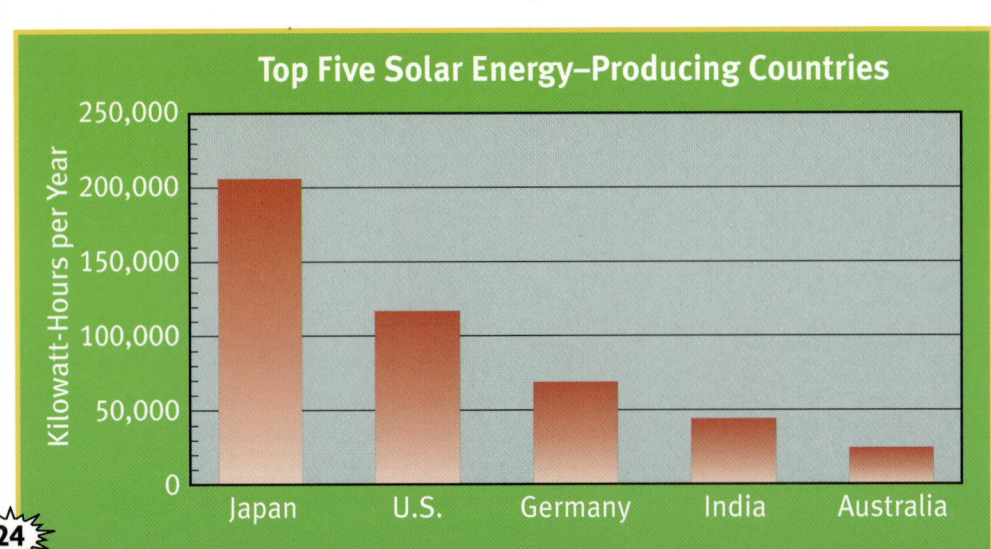

Top Five Solar Energy–Producing Countries

Country	Kilowatt-Hours per Year
Japan	~205,000
U.S.	~115,000
Germany	~70,000
India	~45,000
Australia	~25,000

SOLAR, WIND, GEOTHERMAL, AND BIOMASS ENERGY

Wind Energy

The wind is another renewable source of energy. Wind turbines are used to capture the wind's energy. The wind turns the blades of the turbine. The turbine then spins a generator that produces electricity. Large groups of turbines are called wind farms or wind parks. Wind farms can be built offshore to take advantage of strong ocean winds.

Germany and Spain use wind power more than any other countries do. Thirty states in the United States have wind power projects. California generates the most electricity from wind power. Texas is the second largest producer.

This wind farm in Germany generates enough energy to power a whole town.

Science in the News

Plans for a wind farm off the shore of Cape Cod in Massachusetts have stirred much debate. The wind farm would have 130 wind turbines that are 40 stories high. Some people like the idea of clean energy. Others say the wind farm would be harmful to sea birds, shellfish, and sea mammals. Some fear the farm would ruin the beauty of the coast.

CHAPTER 4

Wind power doesn't pollute the environment. But it does have some harmful effects. Birds and bats are killed when they fly into the turbines' spinning blades. Large wind farms also interfere with the migration routes of some birds.

✓ Point

Talk It Over

What do you think about the effects of wind power on animals? Talk about the question with a friend.

a wind turbine in Wyoming

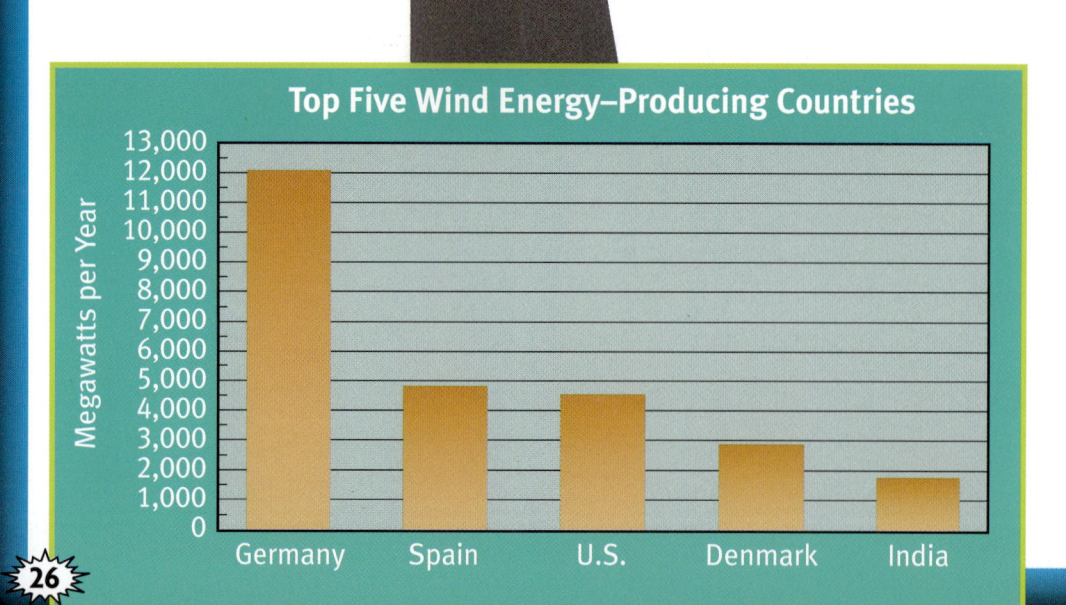

Top Five Wind Energy–Producing Countries

Country	Megawatts per Year
Germany	12,000
Spain	4,800
U.S.	4,500
Denmark	2,800
India	1,700

SOLAR, WIND, GEOTHERMAL, AND BIOMASS ENERGY

IT'S A FACT

About 85 percent of the buildings in Iceland are heated with geothermal energy.

People swim in heated water next to a geothermal energy plant in Iceland.

Geothermal Energy

Geothermal energy is a renewable resource from heat inside Earth. Beneath Earth's crust is a layer of hot, liquid rock called **magma**. Magma is what rises up in a volcano when it erupts. While magma is still underground, it heats pools of underground water. The hot water and steam from such pools can be used to heat buildings. This hot water and steam can also be used to turn the turbines of power plants and generate electricity.

Most countries that use geothermal energy are in parts of the world with active volcanoes. Iceland and Japan are two of these countries. Some Japanese cities even run hot-water pipes under roads to melt snow.

CHAPTER 4

In the United States, the use of geothermal energy is confined mostly to states in the West. Fourteen regions in California use this form of energy.

Geothermal energy plants don't take up as much space as wind farms. The energy plants cause little harm to the environment. The emissions they send into the air are just a tiny fraction of the emissions caused by burning fossil fuels.

Not many places in the world can use geothermal energy. The geological conditions must be just right.

A geyser of hot water and steam erupts in Iceland.

The magma and pools of water must be there. and they can't be too far under the ground.

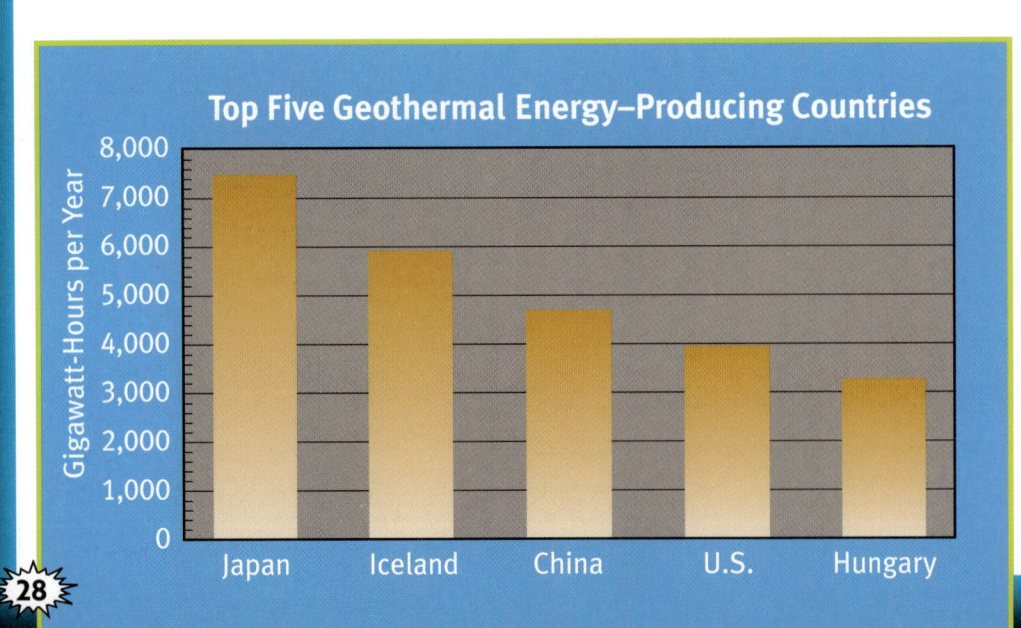

Top Five Geothermal Energy–Producing Countries

Country	Gigawatt-Hours per Year
Japan	7,500
Iceland	5,900
China	4,700
U.S.	4,000
Hungary	3,300

Biomass Energy

Biomass is another renewable energy resource. Biomass includes wood, sawdust, straw, and manure. When these wastes are burned, they give off heat. In some parts of the world, biomass is burned to heat homes.

Certain food crops, like sugar cane, can be used as biomass. Some parts of corn plants can be used to make a fuel called ethanol (EHTH-uh-nawl). Gasoline causes less air pollution when it is mixed with ethanol.

IT'S A FACT

Cow manure is a common biomass fuel in India. People collect cow manure and put it in a device outside their house called a biogas plant. This device separates methane gas from the manure. The gas then runs through hoses into the house, where the gas is used to power lamps and cooking stoves.

Some of the world's power plants use biomass to produce electricity. In the United States, only about 3 percent of electricity is generated by biomass.

A woman collects cow manure to use in a biogas plant.

Conclusion

Each energy resource has good points and bad points. Fossil fuels are the least expensive resource. But are they worth the pollution they cause? Will there be enough fossil fuels to meet future energy demands? Experts predict that known oil reserves could run out in about 80 years.

Water used to generate hydropower is renewable. But what about the impact dams have on people and wildlife? Solar energy sounds ideal, but solar technology is still costly.

Because the world's population is constantly growing, the demand for energy is growing, too. How will we meet our need for energy resources in the future?

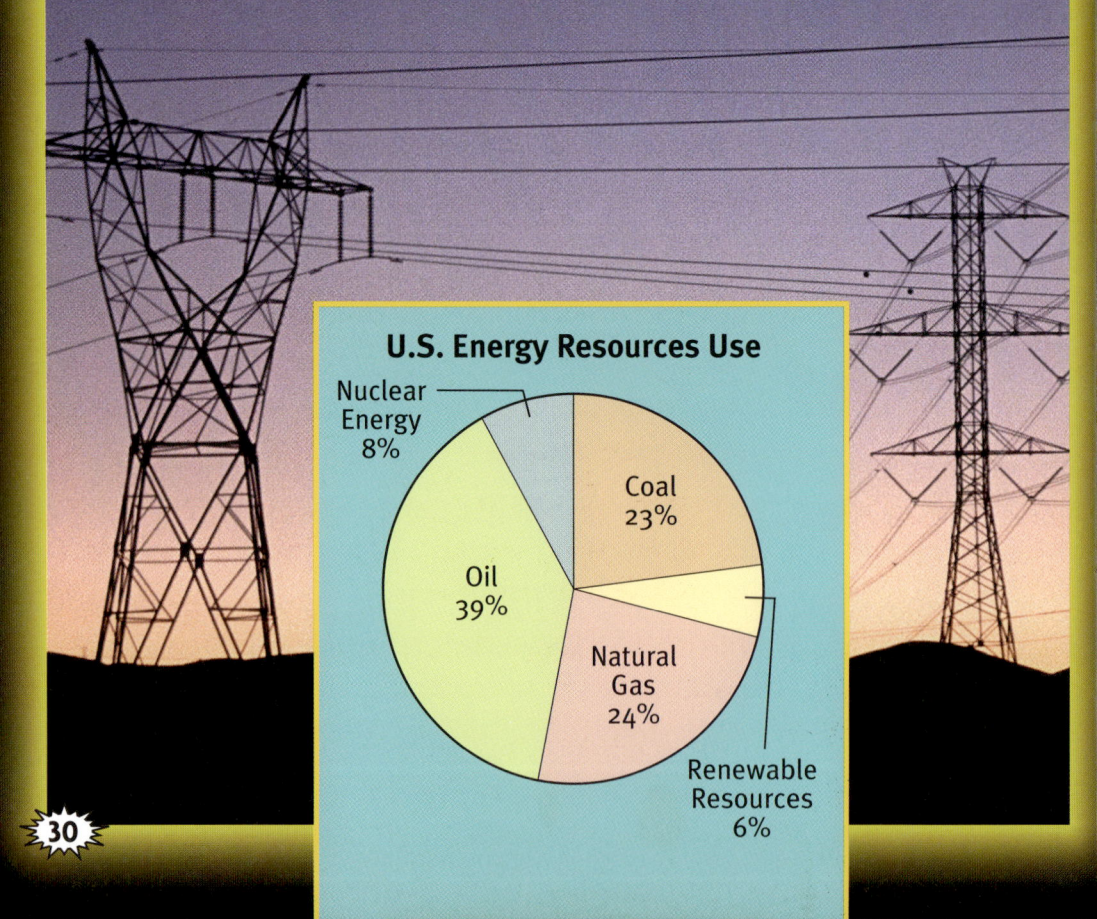

U.S. Energy Resources Use

- Nuclear Energy 8%
- Coal 23%
- Oil 39%
- Natural Gas 24%
- Renewable Resources 6%

Glossary

biomass — (BIGH-oh-mas) plant materials and animal waste used as a source of fuel (page 29)

emission — (ee-MIH-shuhn) something that is given off or sent out; smoke is an emission from a fire (page 12)

fossil fuel — (FOS-uhl fyool) fuel that was formed from the remains of plants and other organisms (page 4)

generator — (JEHN-er-ay-ter) an engine that changes mechanical energy into electrical energy (page 18)

geothermal energy — (jee-oh-THER-muhl EHN-er-jee) energy from the heat inside Earth (page 27)

hydropower — (HIGH-droh-pow-er) power generated by the force of water (page 18)

magma — (MAG-muh) the hot, liquid rock that rises up inside a volcano; it is called lava when it flows out of the volcano (page 27)

nonrenewable resource — (non-ree-NOO-uh-buhl REE-sors) a resource that cannot be replaced when it is used up (page 2)

radiation — (ray-dee-AY-shuhn) energy given off by the nucleus of an atom in the form of particles or rays (page 16)

radioactive waste — (RAY-dee-oh-AK-tihv WAYST) waste from a nuclear power plant (page 16)

renewable resource — (ree-NOO-uh-buhl REE-sors) a resource that is constantly renewed; the Sun and the wind are renewable resources (page 2)

reserve — (rih-ZERV) a known deposit of energy resources (page 6)

solar energy — (SOH-ler EHN-er-jee) energy from the Sun (page 23)

Index

biomass, 29

Chernobyl, 17

Clean Air Act, 12

coal, 2, 4–5, 10, 12, 14, 26, 30

dam, 18–21, 30

electricity, 2–3, 4, 9, 10, 14–15, 18–19, 23–26, 27, 29

emissions, 12, 28

environment, 16, 20, 22, 26, 28

Exxon Valdez, 13

fission, 15

fossil fuel, 4–13, 22, 28, 30

fry grease, 12

generator, 18, 25

geologist, 6

geothermal energy 27–28

global warming, 11

greenhouse gas, 11

hydropower, 18–21, 30

natural gas, 2, 4–6, 8–9, 30

nonrenewable resource, 2, 4, 16

nuclear energy, 14–17, 30

oil, 2, 4–7, 8–9, 13, 30

pollution, 9, 13, 15, 20, 26, 29, 30

radioactive waste, 16–17

renewable resource, 3, 20, 22, 25, 27, 29, 30

reserve, 6–8, 30

solar cell, 23

solar energy, 23–24, 30

solar panel, 23

Three Gorges Dam, 19, 21

Three Mile Island, 17

turbine, 18, 25–26, 27

uranium, 14–16

watt, 3

wind energy, 25–26

wind turbine, 25–26